MINNESOTA ICE
ARENAS

Mike Krieter

THIS PAGE - The Shattuck St. Mary's Arena in Faribault was an impressive wood structure when first completed back in 1967.

Created by Mike Krieter

© 2007 Mike Krieter Photos, 6302 Rose Court, Edina, MN 55424

www.minnesotaicearenas.com

ISBN 978-0-9787956-3-4

Library of Congress Control # 2007937916

Printed by **CATALYST GRAPHICS, INC.**
PRINTING AND BINDING SOLUTIONS
Mark Burgeson 651-452-2403 ext. 23

First printing Fall 2007

Published by D Media Inc. 4601 Excelsior Blvd. #301, Minneapolis, MN 55416
dmedia@juno.com

Publisher of **the *Minnesota* series**

Look for *Storms* and the rest of the series in book stores and on the net at www.adventurepublications.net

STORMS!
Tales of Extreme Weather Events in Minnesota

By Martin Keller and Sheri O'Meara
With Foreword by Belinda Jensen

the *Minnesota* series

COVER PHOTO - The State Fair Coliseum during a Bantam district game in January 2006.

MINNESOTA ICE

ARENAS

Mike Krieter

Don Beaupre was born in Ontario and spent 17 years as an NHL goalie with the Minnesota North Stars, Washington Capitals, Ottawa Senators and Toronto Maple Leafs. Beaupre, a two-time All Star, retired in 1997, returning to Minnesota where he often makes it to the rinks as a father and coach for his children's teams, and as an Assistant Coach for Edina High School.

As time goes by, we definitely grow older and hopefully grow wiser. Though our ability to recall past events has a tendency to fail us at times, it is our memory that allows us to recreate special moments that have had the most impact on our lives.

For me, hours spent playing hockey at the local Waterloo Memorial Arena impacted me in ways I appreciate more as the years pass. There wasn't anything glamorous about the arena but it holds the fondest memories I have of all my hockey-playing years because it's where I started. For the Minnesota hockey player, parent, coach, referee or fan, hearing the names of the great old and not so old ice arenas in the state of Minnesota likely brings back similar memories of time spent in the arenas that helped shape players, communities, and the state as one of the richest in hockey tradition.

"Minnesota Ice Arenas" is a collection of images of the arenas where a lot of great hockey moments of the past have taken place. These are the places where we may have scored our first goal, coached in a championship game, or watched a future NHL star develop his skills. These are community ice rinks where kids start out skating with the innocence of simply loving to play the game. Just like Waterloo Arena was for me.

The crisp air, the smell of popcorn and hot dogs, and the crack of the puck echoing off the boards are all part of fond memories spent at the hockey rink. I hope the following pages help you to recall special moments you've spent in Minnesota's Ice Arenas!

DON BEAUPRE

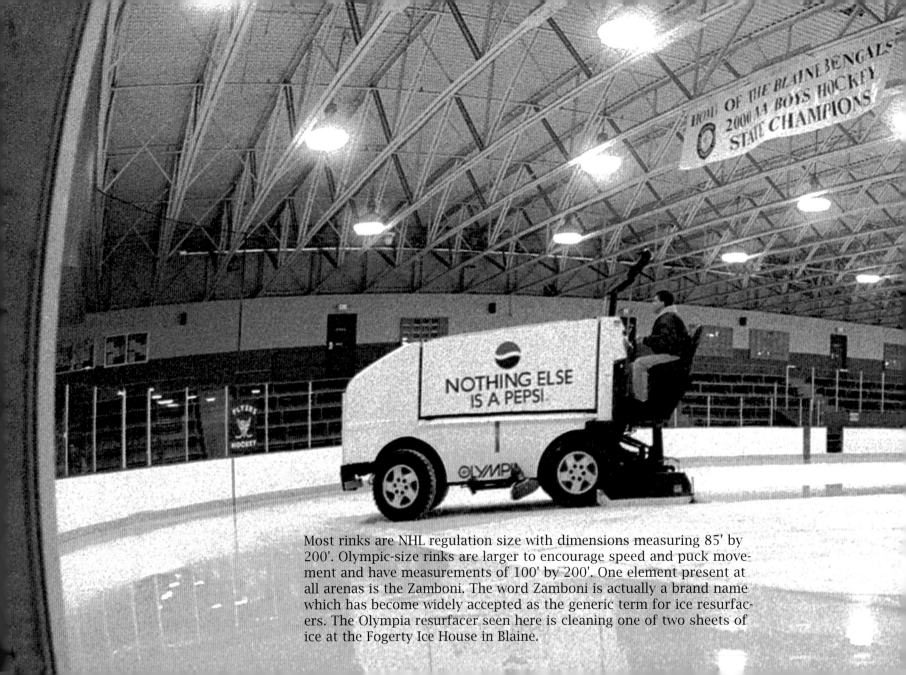

Most rinks are NHL regulation size with dimensions measuring 85' by 200'. Olympic-size rinks are larger to encourage speed and puck movement and have measurements of 100' by 200'. One element present at all arenas is the Zamboni. The word Zamboni is actually a brand name which has become widely accepted as the generic term for ice resurfacers. The Olympia resurfacer seen here is cleaning one of two sheets of ice at the Fogerty Ice House in Blaine.

About the Minnesota Ice Arenas Book

Is Minnesota really the State of Hockey? If the number of indoor ice arenas is any measure, then the answer would be yes. With 173 separate facilities, totaling 245 covered indoor rinks, Minnesota leads the nation in refrigerated ice.

I grew up in Minnesota playing hockey. Years later my three children would also play. Thousands of ice times later, it felt as if I had been to every single arena in the state. This thought started me pondering about just how many indoor arenas there were, and the idea for the book was born. I would visit and photograph each and every one.

After collecting a list of arenas, I planned my attack, and started driving. Every building had its own personality, history and story to tell. I found myself anticipating what my next rink adventure would reveal as I made my way around the (rather large I might add) state of Minnesota.

The images to follow were mostly gathered in my trek around Minnesota the winter of 2006-07. I also included a handful of photos that were collected along the way during my children's events.

My approach, when shooting an arena, was to take pictures of whatever was going on or not going on when I was there. The results were pictures of games, practices, figure skating, open skating and plenty of empty sheets of ice. A couple locations were not open when I scheduled my visit and is the reason for missing interior photos. I apologize if I mistakenly overlooked any arena, but I made an attempt to locate as many as I could.

Take a look at the arenas in this book and enjoy revisiting ones you already know, and get a glimpse of the ones that you haven't made it to...yet.

Mike Krieter

MAJOR HISTORICAL MINNESOTA RINKS

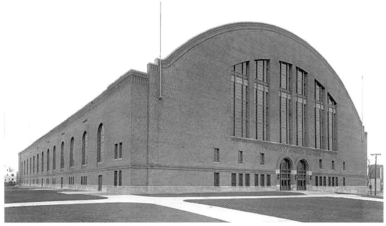

Williams Arena at the University of Minnesota was known as the "Barn" and was the home of the Gophers until 1985, when they took up residence in the new Mariucci Arena.

The Metropolitan Sports Center was completed in 1967 and served as home for a number of teams, most notably the Minnesota North Stars until their relocation to Dallas in 1993. The building was demolished in 1994 and is now the location of the Ikea store neighboring the Mall of America in Bloomington.

The Minneapolis Arena operated from 1925 to 1963 and served as home ice for the Gophers during the '20s to the '50s. Pictured here is the 1925 Minneapolis vs. St. Paul game for the Kiwanian's National Convention.

The Saint Paul Auditorium, renamed the Roy Wilkins Auditorium in 1985, was built in 1936. The Gophers used it as one of their home rinks until the '50s. The Minnesota Fighting Saints of the short-lived WHA (World Hockey Association) used it in the fall of 1972 before they took up residence in their new home, the St. Paul Civic Center.

The St. Paul Civic Center was built in 1972 as a home for the Minnesota Fighting Saints of the WHA. The team lasted only until 1977 and the WHA folded the next season. The Civic Center served as the site for the High School Hockey State Tournament until 1998 when it was torn down to make way for the Xcel Center. The Civic Center may be best known for its unique clear boards. The clear board idea never caught on, possibly due in part to the fact that it eliminates prime advertising space.

Chaska Community Center Rink 2
during a Squirt Tournament game.

THE ARENAS

This book is arranged alphabetically by location/city and then by arena name within that city. There also is a simple map at the back of this book with location and corresponding page number for each of the arenas.

ALBERT LEA   CITY ARENA

No toe picks on these rental skates.

The main arena is a classic wood one and the second arena is a modern metal structure.

Rink 2

Albert Lea City Arena
701 Lake Chapeau Dr.
Albert Lea, MN 56007

507-377-4374

NOTES - This is a 2-sheet facility, with
the first being built 1974. It is the home
of the Albert Lea High School Panthers
and the Albert Lea Hockey Association.

The City Arena is actually
out in the country.

The St. Michael-Albertville Youth Hockey Association skates on a February 2007 Saturday morning.

STMA Arena
5898 Lachman Ave.
Albertville, MN 55301

763-497-6749

NOTES - Recently built in 1998, with a 2006 locker room expansion, this 1-rink facility is home for the St. Michael-Albertville Knights Boys HS Hockey Team as well as the North Wright County River Hawks Girls High School Co-op. It is conveniently located near the Albertville Outlet Mall.

13

What a spread!

Runestone Community Center
802 3rd Ave. W.
Alexandria, MN 56308

320-763-4466

NOTES - The wooden West Rink was built in 1978 and the East Rink added later. This is the home of the Alexandria High School Cardinals and the Youth Hockey Association.

ANDOVER

ANDOVER COMMUNITY CENTER ARENA

Andover CC Arena
1685 Crosstown Blvd.
Andover, MN 55304

763-767-5100

NOTES - Andover's single-sheet ice rink is part of the Andover Community Center complex and is home to the Andover High School Huskies. It's a regulation rink with a 1250-spectator capacity. The facility is a joint operation between the City of Andover and the YMCA. The City operates the ice arena and field house. The YMCA operates the fitness area, studios and two swimming pools.

15

3:30PM - Rink 1 gets ready for the High School Boys Team to practice.

Rink 2 waits quietly for its next event.

Anoka Area Ice Arena
4111 7th Ave. N.
Anoka, MN 55303

763-427-8163

NOTES - This 2-rink complex was built in 1981 and is home to Anoka High School Hockey Teams.

APPLE VALLEY

Hayes Park Arena
14595 Hayes Rd.
Apple Valley, MN 55124

952-953-2366

NOTES - Hayes Park is just across the street from the High School. This 1-sheet arena was built in 1995 as added ice for Apple Valley and Eastview. It seats approximately 200.

Apple Valley U14 A takes on Edina in 2006.

APPLE VALLEY

APPLE VALLEY SPORTS ARENA

Apple Valley Sports Arena
14452 Hayes Rd.
Apple Valley, MN 55124

952-953-2366

The crowd filters in for an Apple Valley Girls High School game in November.

NOTES - Built in 1976, this rink provides ice for Apple Valley and Eastview High Schools as well as both communities' Youth Hockey Associations. The rink is connected to the high school and it seats about 1000.

"What's good?" Well, everything if you had to come straight from work.

17

AUSTIN

PACKER ARENA

Packer Arena
607 7th St. N.E.
Austin, MN 55912

507-433-1881

NOTES - The Packer arena sits just a block from the older Austin Riverside Arena and was just recently completed. Athough it's a newer facility, it seats just 250 and the High School still competes in the Riverside Arena.

The Packer Arena seen here during a January Tournament game.

AUSTIN

RIVERSIDE ARENA

Riverside Arena
501 2nd Ave. NE
Austin, MN 55912

507-433-1881

NOTES - Built in 1978, this rink seats 2500 and serves the Austin High School. In the summer it hosts a number of dry floor activities including concerts and boat & RV shows.

BABBIT

BABBIT ARENA

Babbit Arena
4077 Highway 21
Babbit, MN 55732

218-827-3471

NOTES - This small Iron Range town built the Babbit Arena in 1967, which sits next to the Babbit High School.

BAGLEY

A. F. KAISER ARENA

A. F. Kaiser Arena
36283 Fairground Rd.
Bagley, MN 56621

218-694-3178

NOTES - Built in 1996 by the Youth Hockey Association, this rink sits on the fairgrounds and is home to Bagley High School Hockey.

19

BAUDETTE

Spectators filter in for the start of a Bantam game.

Rink 2 is bare bones, using the main rink's locker rooms.

A heated spectator area provides comfortable viewing.

Baudette Arena
303 5th St. S.W.
Baudette, MN 56623

218-634-1319

NOTES - This arena is about as far north as Minnesota gets, sitting near Lake of the Woods. It was built in 1978 and is a 2-sheet facility. This is home ice for the Lake of the Woods High School Bears.

20

This river rink in Baudette played host to the Baudette Bay Pond Hockey Classic, which was held in January 2007 and featured the Lake of the Woods High School Bears vs. the St. Paul Johnson Governors.

BEMIDJI

BEMIDJI COMMUNITY ARENA

Bemidji Community Arena
3000 Division St. W.
Bemidji, MN 56601

218-444-5661

NOTES - Completed in 2001, this arena neighbors the Bemidji High School.

Don't forget to take a picture with Paul Bunyan and Babe the Blue Ox.

BEMIDJI

JOHN GLAS FIELDHOUSE

John Glas Fieldhouse
1500 Birchmont Dr. N.W.
Bemidji, MN 56601

218-755-2944

NOTES - This arena was built in 1967 and sits on the Bemidji State University. It plays host to both the Men and Women D1 BSU Hockey Teams.

Judging from the name tags, BSU has many loyal season-ticket holders.

BEMIDJI

NOTES - The 1-sheet ice rink facility built in 1967 was not open when I was there, but the attached Curling Club was hopping.

NEILSON-REISE ARENA

Neilson-Reise Arena
23rd St. & Ash Ave.
Bemidji, MN 56601

218-751-4541

BEMIDJI

NYMORE ARENA

Nymore Arena
3rd St. & Pershing Ave.
Bemidji, MN 56601

218-751-4541

NOTES - The Nymore Arena has one sheet of ice and was built in 1972 by the School District for the High School Team.

Benson Civic Cener Arena
2200 Tatges Ave.
Benson, MN 56215

320-843-4377

NOTES - This single-sheet facility was built in 1994 by the City of Benson for the High School and local Association.

These photos were shot just prior to a Benson Boys High School Hockey game. One loyal fan arrives early to claim the center bleacher seat in the heated viewing area.

BLAINE   FOGERTY ARENA

NOTES - Built in 1982 by
Spring Lake Park and
Blaine School Districts, this
2-sheet facility plays host
to both of their High
School teams.

The U14 South Team gets
some last-minute instruction
before the start of the championship game in the Midwest
Selects AAA Hockey
Tournament, August 2006. The
team would go on to win the
game in decisive fashion.

Fogerty Arena
9250 Lincoln St. N.E.
Blaine, MN 55434

763-780-3328

With rinks 1-4 spiraling out from this central hub, the Super Rink makes for a superb tournament venue.

Schwan Super Rink
1700 10th Ave. NE
Blaine, MN 55449

763-717-3880

NOTES - The Super Rink is the largest indoor hockey facility in the world. It has eight sheets of ice: The first four Olympic-size rinks were built in 1998 and the last four NHL size rinks were completed winter of 2006-07. The first of its kind, Herb Brooks Training Center is also located within the facility.

The Herb Brooks Training Center.

One of the original four Olympic-size rinks during the Stick It To Cancer Tournament, April 2005.

Rinks 5-8 are NHL regulation-size sheets.

BLOOMINGTON ICE GARDEN

Bloomington Jefferson High School Girls Team practices on Rink 3 after school.

Mom takes notes during a figure skating session on Rink 2.

Bloomington Ice Garden
3600 W. 98th St.
Bloomington, MN 55431

952-563-8842

NOTES - The original Rink 1 was built in 1970 with two more sheets being added later, including the Olympic-size Rink 3.

An Edina Squirt Team takes the ice for a District game on Rink 2.

The puck drops at a Squirt Tournament game, January 2001.

Brainerd Civic Center
502 Jackson St.
Brainerd, MN 56401

218-825-3005

NOTES - This is a two-regulation-sheet facility. The first one, built in 1977, was the Civic Center Arena which has viewing for approximately 900. The second, Gold Medal Arena, was completed in 1999 with seating for just 200. This arena is home to the Brainerd Warrior High School Teams, and also hosts numerous tournaments each season.

There is plenty of ice at nearby Lake Mille Lacs.

30

BREEZY POINT

Taking the ice for a Bantam
Tournament game, 2005.

That's a fine rink menu.

Time out with 45 seconds left, a man advantage and two goals down...always exciting!

Breezy Point Sports Arena
9252 Breezy Point Dr.
Breezy Point, MN 56472

218-562-5678

NOTES - Breezy Point Arena, built in 1999, is just outside Brainerd and ideal for tournaments with Breezy Point Resort nearby.

31

Edina U12 A prepares for a District Playoff game, February 2005.

Brooklyn Park Ice Arenas
5600 85th Ave. N.
Brooklyn Park, MN 55443

763-493-8333

NOTES - This is a two-regulation-size rink facility. The first one built was the Brooklyn Park Ice Arena 1, which was completed in 1983 and seats 800. The second Dennis C. Palm Arena which followed in 1997 seats 300. The Park Center High School North Metro Stars consider this home ice. Local players of note include Krissy Wendell, Trent Klatt and Casey Borer.

Peterson Rink during a Girls High School Team practice, December 2006.

Younger siblings watching Buffalo Boys High School Team run through a practice on the Civic Center Rink.

Buffalo Civic Center
1306 County Rd. 134
Buffalo, MN 55313

763-682-4132

NOTES - The Peterson Rink was built in 1977 with the Civic Center being added in 2001, with seating for 1200. Buffalo High School and Association, as well as the Thunderbirds Womens Hockey Team, call this ice home.

Rink 2 is made ready for the next game.

Rink 1 has seating for 1400.

A view from the players' box in Rink 2.

Burnsville Ice Center
251 Civic Center Pkwy.
Burnsville, MN 55337

952-895-4651

NOTES - The Burnsville Ice Center was built in 1972. Though they look similar, Rink 1 building is slightly larger to accommodate stands and is where the Burnsville High School Boys and Girls Teams play.

These photos were shot in March 2007. The High School and Association's seasons were complete, leaving a whole lot of ice time for the youngsters.

Four Seasons Sports Arena
1568 Highway 210
Carlton, MN 55718

218-384-3227

NOTES - Built in 1996 by the Carlton Hockey Association, this single rink facility is home to the Carlton High School Bulldogs.

The Ice Forum
12165 Ensign Ave.
Champlin, MN 55316

763-421-3696

NOTES - Built in 1996, this single-sheet complex offers pleasant common areas which make it the place to be any night of the week.

A delayed penalty is called during a 2001 Squirt District game in Rink 2.

NOTES - This 2-rink facility was built in 1991 as part of a sports center with gymnasiums, a pool and other resources. Rink 1 is used as an indoor soccer field during the summer months with Rink 2 keeping ice year 'round.

Chaska Community Center
1661 Park Ridge Dr.
Chaska, MN 55318

952-448-5633

Rink 1 grows turf during the summer months.

Sports Arena
600 1st St. N.W.
Chisholm, MN 55719

218-254-7919

NOTES - This single-sheet complex was built
in 1972 and recently received a big
makeover including new lighting, plexiglass,
a nice paint job and a reflective ceiling.

To find the rink, simply head to
the water tower.

The lobby of the arena says it all:
This Iron Range town loves their
hockey.

CIRCLE PINES   CENTENNIAL SPORTS ARENA

This is a very strong hockey community as seen by the banners and the practice jersey worn by this Centennial player.

Centennial Sports Arena
4707 North Rd.
Circle Pines, MN 55014

763-792-6090

NOTES - This single-rink arena is situated at Centennial High School and was built in 1992 for the Centennial Cougars. It also provides ice for the local Association. Players of note, both going onto the U of M and beyond, include RJ Anderson (Philadelphia) and Ryan Flynn (Nashville). The arena keeps ice June to March, then it has a short turf season March and April.

Pine Valley Arena in foreground and the newer Rec. Center in background.   Edina HS Girls play Cloquet in the Barn, 2006.

Cloquet Area Rec. Center
1102 Olympic Dr.
Cloquet, MN 55720

218-879-5400

NOTES - The original Pine Valley Arena is classic old-time hockey. The rink size is an odd 185' X 85' and the arena was originally open on the sidewalls to the elements. It seats a surprisingly large number of spectators, maxing out at 1200 (with no seat more than about 20' from the glass). It provided ice for Cloquet High School until the newer Rec. Center rink was built in 1997. The Rec. Center sheet also has odd dimensions, measuring in at 200' X 90'.

The newer Rec. Center Arena seats 2400.

AND PINE VALLEY ARENA

Get set to take a step back in time when entering the "Barn," as Pine Valley Arena is affectionately known by the locals.

Original wood truss roof system and wood benches.

Hodgins-Berardo Arena
200 Curley Ave.
Coleraine, MN 55722

218-245-3525

NOTES - This is a classic old arena built back in 1962. When
full to its capacity of 2000 fans cheering on the Greenway
High School Team, you know they live hockey around here.

COON RAPIDS

JOE COOK MEMORIAL ARENA

Coon Rapids Cardinals Junior Gold controls the puck during a game against Edina, 2007.

Joe Cook Memorial Arena
11091 Mississippi Blvd.
Coon Rapids, MN 55433

762-421-5035

NOTES - Built in 1973, this arena
plays host to Coon Rapids High
School, Youth Association and
Anoka Ramsey Community College.

Cottage Grove Ice Arena
8020 80th St. S.
Cottage Grove, MN 55016

651-458-3400

NOTES - This arena sits next to Park High School and was built in 1974. The main rink is regulation, seating 1200, with a second smaller studio rink measuring 120' X 65'. A third rink is scheduled for completion in August of 2008. Park High School Hockey calls this home, and starting in 2009, so will East Ridge High School.

Rink 1 during a Park High School Boys practice session.

The Civic Rink was added later.

The Sports Arena has the original 1937 wood truss barrel roof overhead.

Crookston Civic Arena
220 Robert St. E.
Crookston, MN 56716

218-281-2465

NOTES - The original rink in the foreground was built in 1937 with smaller dimensions of 180' X 80'.

CROSBY

HALLETT CENTER ARENA

Hallett Center Arena
470 8th St. N.E.
Crosby, MN 56441

218-546-2616

NOTES - Built in 1999, this is a single regulation-size rink seating 330. Crosby-Ironton-Aitkin Lightning High School and Association, as well as the Brainerd Lakes Curling Club, use this ice. Former employee Ace Slepica currently plays with the USAF All Star Hockey Team in Germany.

DELANO

DELANO AREA ICE ARENA

Delano Area Ice Arena
654 Tiger Dr.
Delano, MN 55328

763-972-6478

NOTES - Home of Delano Tiger High School and Association Hockey, this 1-sheet arena built in 1990 also plays host to spirited "Old Man" games. The picture here shows some of Delano's parents warming up for a game.

Rink 2 waits for the next event.

The old guys on the bench will tell you that the far boards, against the cement wall, are a killer.

Kent Freeman Arena
1300 Rossman Ave.
Detroit Lakes, MN 56506

218-847-7738

NOTES - Rink 1 was built in 1966 with slightly small ice dimensions of 195' X 84'. The old timers don't fill the stands like the High School Team.

47

DULUTH

The historic William A. Irwin is docked across the street and is open for tours May through October.

January 24, 2007, the UMD Bulldogs are driving to the net with the score tied during the second period of a game with the Northern Michigan Wildcats.

DECC
350 Harbor Dr.
Duluth, MN 55802

218-722-5573

The DECC from the lake side.

NOTES - The DECC sits down in Canal Park in Duluth; it was built back in 1966. It has two sheets of ice with both being slightly undersized at 190' X 85'. It plays host to the powerhouse University of Minnesota Duluth Bulldogs and the local High Schools.

Just moments later, the Bulldogs score a goal to go up 2-1.

The High Bridge with steam rising from Lake Superior on a sub-zero January morning.

The rag on the Zamboni says it all....dress warm.

Fryberger Arena
3211 Alladale Ave.
Duluth, MN 55803

218-724-0094

NOTES - This single-sheet arena was built in 1972 to service Duluth East High School and local Associations.

Old-time hand-painted advertising is everywhere.

An Association Team works some 2-on-1 drills.

The radio towers turn the sky red on this snowy night, January 2007.

Mars Lakeview Arena
1215 Rice Lake Rd.
Duluth, MN 55811

218-722-4455

NOTES - This is a 1-sheet arena and is the home of Marshall Hilltoppers who frequently make their way to the State High School Tournament.

Smiles everyone. Edina U14 A poses for a team photo after winning the 2006 Icebreaker Tournament.

UMD Arena
10 University Dr.
Duluth, MN 55810

218-726-7387

NOTES - Completed in 1986, this rink sits in a multi-sport complex right in the middle of the UMD campus. It serves as the practice rink for both Men and Women Bulldogs. They play their games at the DECC.

Some duct tape will fix that clock controller right up.

The main arena.

The second arena during an Eagan vs. Edina Junior Gold game, 2007.

Eagan Civic Center
3870 Pilot Knob Rd.
Eagan, MN 55122

651-675-5590

NOTES - Built in 1995, this 2-rink facility services both Eagan and Apple Valley (Eastview) High Schools and Associations.

Little brother finds something to do during ice time.

East Bethel Ice Arena
20675 Hwy. 65
East Bethel, MN 55011

763-434-7579

NOTES - This rink was built in 1995 and is home to the St. Francis Fighting Saints. That is the same name as the former Minnesota professional WHA Hockey Team, and if you look at the logo on the wall, it's the same logo as well.

54

March 2007, the High School season may be over but the young ones keep practicing for next year.

A Peewee game gets underway, 2007.

When full to its 2500 seating capacity during High School games, this arena rocks.

East Grand Forks Civic Center
300 15th St. N.E.
East Grand Forks, MN 56721

218-773-9073

NOTES - This 1-sheet arena was built
in 1974 as a home for the East
Grand Forks High School Team.

Sisters come to cheer at this U10 Girls Association game.

Taking the ice.

Rink 2.

VFW Memorial Youth Center
711 3rd St. S.E.
East Grand Forks, MN 56721

218-773-9073

NOTES - This 2-rink facility was completed in 1982 by volunteers including the Blue Line Club. In 1987 it was turned over to the city. The entire area was flooded in April of 1997 and this arena was under 42" of water. By the next winter however, the rink was up and running with a new compressor, boards, all new electrical and topped off with a fresh coat of paint.

Eden Prairie's second rink is Olympic size, seen here during open skating.

Player boxes are tight in the Main Rink.

The Main Rink during a Bantam game, 2006.

Eden Prairie Community Center
16700 Valley View Rd.
Eden Prairie, MN 55346

952-949-8470

NOTES - The first rink, EP Main, was built in 1982 with the third sheet being completed for use in 2007, as this book comes out.

4-on-4 and 3-on-3 leagues are very popular at Velocity because of the small sheet size.

Velocity Hockey Center
7901 Fuller Rd.
Eden Prairie, MN 55344

952-937-0949

NOTES - This facility opened in 2005 originally as The Pond, and is a single reduced-size
sheet measuring 130' X 65'.

Authentic signed hockey memorabilia
fills the lobby area.

A new crop of players watch the game.

The West Arena during a Girls High School Hornets game, 2007.

Braemar's South Rink.

Braemar Arena
7501 Ikola Way
Edina, MN 55439

952-941-1322

NOTES - Braemar Arena started out in 1965 with one sheet of ice and now has three sheets which are in use year 'round. Edina was known through the '70s as a Hockey Dynasty, and leads in the High School record books with nine State Championships. In total, Edina holds 32 state titles between High School and Association Teams.

59

Braemar's West Arena was impressive for its day; built back in 1965, it seats 3600 comfortably.

EDINA   MINNESOTA MADE ICE CENTER

Lets play hockey! MN Made is open and operating.

MN Made under construction in November of 2006.

Edina Girls JV practices on Rink 1, December 2006. With ice in high demand, Edina and other communities fill their schedules with ice time at MN Made.

Rink 1 during a District Junior Gold game, January 2007.

NOTES - This private venture by Minnesota Made, in 2006, adds three regulation rinks to an area where there is a shortage of indoor ice during regular season play. It is home to MN Made Hockey Schools as well as the Edina Curling Club, pictured here on Rink 2. These structures housed the old Midwest Tennis Club and provided cost effective buildings in which to create this new facility.

Minnesota Made Ice Center
7300 Bush Lake Rd.
Edina, MN 55439

952-746-5728

61

An Elk River Peewee team practices in the Olympic Rink.

A mom looks on in the Barn.

The lobby sports Elk River red and black.

Elk River Ice Arena
1000 School St.
Elk River, MN 55330

763-635-1140

NOTES - The Barn rink was built back in 1972 and the Olympic added later.

Banners on the front of the arena show NHL players who grew up on this ice, including Joel Otto, Dan Hinote and Paul Martin.

The glass shows some serious use.

High school girls watch the boys.

Ely High School Boys Team runs through some drills after school.

Ely's main street is a wintery scene.

Trucks seem to be the preferred vehicle to get to the rink.

Ely Ice Arena
600 E. Harvey St.
Ely, MN 55731

218-365-5041

NOTES - The Ely Ice Arena was built by the School District in 1976 and sits next to the High School.

EVELETH

Getting ready to drop the puck on another Youth Hockey game.

Eveleth boasts the world's largest hockey stick.

The U.S. Hockey Hall of Fame is a must see site in Eveleth.

Eveleth Hippodrome
611 Douglas Ave.
Eveleth, MN 55734

218-744-5566

NOTES - Originally built back in 1930, and with seating for 3000, the Eveleth Hippodrome has hosted many major Iron Range High School battles.

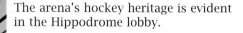

The arena's hockey heritage is evident in the Hippodrome lobby.

FAIRMONT

MARTIN COUNTY ARENA

Martin County Arena
1300 N. Bixby Rd.
Fairmont, MN 56031

507-238-1995

NOTES - This arena is located on Fairmont's Martin County Fairgrounds and was built in 1985 for the High School and local Associations.

FARIBAULT

FARIBAULT ICE ARENA

The Fairmont High School Team runs practice, 2007.

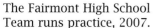

Faribault Ice Arena
1816 2nd Ave. N.W.
Faribault, MN 55021

507-332-0372

NOTES - Completed in recent years, this is a 1-sheet facility located on the Rice County Fairgrounds.

I think that's a winner. A parent tosses one in a "Chuck a Puck" contest during a period break at a Peewee tournament, 2005. Closest to the center dot wins the pot.

FARIBAULT

NOTES - This is a 2-rink facility with the first sheet being built in 1967 and the second in the last several years. It sits on the beautiful Shattuck-St. Mary's campus, which is a prep school known for high-level hockey and churning out one great player after another. Teams bus in from all over to get a chance to play Shattuck.

Shattuck Arena
1000 Shuman Ave.
Faribault, MN 55021

507-333-1664

The original arena is in contrast to the new rink which is complete with concourse seating for the season-ticket holders.

FARMINGTON

FARMINGTON CIVIC ARENA

The Farmington High School Boys Team practices in January 2007.

Farmington Civic Arena
114 W. Spruce St.
Farmington, MN 55024

651-463-2510

NOTES - This 1-sheet facility was built in 1976 for the Farmington High School and Association Teams.

Preparing decorations for the next game.

67

The arena is located on the Otter Tail County Fairgrounds which is just southeast of Fergus Falls.

Fergus Falls Ice Arena
1812 Hwy. 82
Fergus Falls, MN 56537

218-763-2271

NOTES - This 2-sheet arena was built in 1975 with the Main Arena seating 1300. The Satellite Arena is tucked in the back with a smaller sheet measuring 191' X 79'.

FOREST LAKE

MAROON AND GOLD ARENA

Maroon & Gold Arena
832 4th St. S.W.
Forest Lake, MN 55025

651-982-8181

NOTES - Built in 1979, this 1-rink facility serves the Forest Lake High School, Association and Adult League hockey.

GILBERT

DAVID L. SKENZICK ARENA

The rink is squeezed into the building on the right, and it uses the neighboring building for locker rooms, with rubber walking pads between.

NOTES - This modest 1-sheet rink is used by Eveleth/Gilbert High School and Associations. The photo to the left shows the combination of plexiglass, plywood and chain link fence used above the boards for an old-time hockey look.

David L. Skenzick Arena
East Iowa St. & Broadway
Gilbert, MN 55741

218-749-3837

The rules are very simple in this arena.

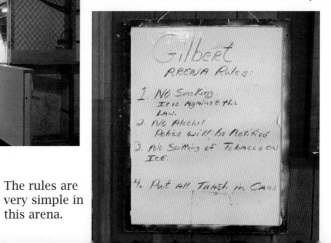

69

High School coach Rob Little puts the Girls Team through its paces.

Breck Boys High School Team practices.

Breck Anderson Arena
4210 Olson Memorial Hwy.
Golden Valley, MN 55422

763-587-0619

NOTES - Breck Anderson Arena opened in 2000 and was built for the Breck High School Boys and Girls Teams. This arena sits about a mile northeast of their previous home, the old Golden Valley Arena, which was demolished when this took its place.

NOTES - This is a 2-rink facility in a big hockey town. The original West Rink (Cliff Kauppi Venue) was built in 1962 and seats 2100. Home teams here include the Grand Rapids Thunderhawks Boys and the Grand Rapids/Greenway Girls High School Teams. Former players here include: Bill Baker (Miracle on Ice 1980 Olympic Team), Don Lucia (U of M Gophers Mens Coach), Chris Marinucci (Hobey Baker Winner and NHL player), Kurt Kleinendorst (Stanley Cup Champion and NJ Devils Coaching Staff), in addition to NHL players Jon Casey, Jon Rohloff, Jeff Neilson, Kirk Nielson and Kelly Fairchild.

Edina U14 A celebrates winning the State Championship in Cliff Kauppi Arena, March 2006.

IRA Civic Center
1401 N.W. 3rd Ave.
Grand Rapids, MN 55744

218-326-2591

The Bill MacDonald Venue was built in 1995 and has Olympic dimensions.

Grand Rapids IRA Civic Center West Rink (Cliff Kauppi Venue) is a great old-time hockey building.

Open skating is on the honor system here.

The dates on this trophy are from the '30s.

Open skating after the High School season.

The banner out front reads *Hallock Hockey Centennial.*

The 2nd Hallock Arena was completed in 1934.

Hallock Ice Arena
201 N. 4th St.
Hallock, MN 56728

218-843-2626

NOTES - Hallock is just a couple miles from both Canada and North Dakota, and is possibly the birth place of Minnesota Hockey. The first indoor arena here was built in 1894; the current Hallock Arena was built in 1974.

Hastings East Arena during a Peewee Tournament game, 2007.

The railing provides premium viewing.

NOTES - The first rink (West Arena) was built in 1974 and seats 900. The second was added in 1997 and seats 200. Players of note from this arena include: Dean Talafous, Bruce Horsch, Brad Doshans, Tom Sagissor, Brad Stephan, John Gruden, Aaron Fox, Luke Gruden, Jeff Taffe, Dan Welch, Tyler Chorney and Michael Gergen.

Hastings Civic Arena
2801 Red Wing Blvd.
Hastings, MN 55033

651-480-6195

The West Arena.

HERMANTOWN

HERMANTOWN ARENA

When the kids are done, the old guys take the ice for a late-night Adult League game.

The concession stand is a hit with guys after an evening game.

The two outdoor rinks provide some extra ice.

NOTES - Hermantown is just outside of Duluth, and this arena has one indoor sheet built in 1988. Hermantown High School Boys Hawks were 2006 State Champions.

Hermantown Arena
4309 Ugstad Rd.
Hermantown, MN 55811

218-729-5493

Parents watch an Association game on a Saturday morning in January 2007.

The Iron Range has a big hockey tradition and some of this is on display in the lobby of the Memorial Arena.

Hibbing Memorial Building Arena
400 E. 23rd St.
Hibbing, MN 55746

218-263-4379

NOTES - This old steel-truss building was built back in 1934. With the ability to seat 3460 and hold an additional 1000 standing, this is the place to be when there is a High School game. The building has seen much over the years including a World Horse Shoe Tournament, the US Curling Nationals and a speech by John F. Kennedy. UMD coach and former NHL player Scott Sandelin grew up on this ice, as well as other NHL players including Pat Micheletti (North Stars), Joel Micheletti (St. Louis), Mike Polich (Montreal) and Bobby Collyard (St. Louis).

Blake Girls HS Varsity vs Edina, 2007.

Blake School Ice Arena
110 Blake Rd.
Hopkins, MN 55343

952-988-3825

NOTES - Blake School Ice Arena is a classic wood structure, with matching wood bleachers, and sits on the Blake Middle School Campus in Hopkins.

77

HOPKINS

HOPKINS PAVILION

Hopkins Pavilion
11000 Excelsior Blvd.
Hopkins, MN 55343

952-939-1410

NOTES - The Pavilion is the
home of the Hopkins High
School Royals and is a single-
sheet arena built in 1962. It
serves as an athletic field
house in the summer months.

They start them young up on the range.

Parents look on during a Sunday morning Mini Mites game in January 2007.

Hoyt Lakes Arena
10 Kennedy Memorial Dr.
Hoyt Lakes, MN 55750

218-225-2226

NOTES - Built in 1970, this single-sheet Iron Range arena services Mesabi East High School and Association Hockey.

Now that's something new, a Mini Mite Girls League.

Burich Arena
950 Harrington St.
Hutchinson, MN 55350

320-234-5640

NOTES - Hutchinson's Burich Arena was built in 1977 with two sheets, and is used by Hutchinson High School and Hockey Association.

INTERNATIONAL FALLS

BRONCO ARENA

Bronco Arena
1515 11th St.
International Falls, MN 56649

218-283-2424

NOTES - Located just a stone's throw from the Canadian border, the Bronco Arena is definitely in hockey country. It is a 1-sheet facility built back in 1969.

INTERNATIONAL FALLS

KERRY PARK ARENA

Kerry Park Arena
International Falls, MN 56649

NOTES - This a 1-sheet facility that I just stumbled upon. Date built is unknown.

The foyer to the arena is spacious and warm and makes for good viewing.

The main East Rink has seating for 1300.

Veterans Memorial CC
8055 Barbara Ave.
Inver Grove Heights, MN 55077

651-450-2514

NOTES - This modern facility was just completed in 1996 with two sheets. It provides ice for Simley High School and Inver Grove Hockey Association.

This photo of the sharpening room, located in the West Rink, was shot through the talk hole in the room's plexiglass window.

The West Rink seen just prior to dropping the puck in a scrimmage between New Prague Girls HS and Edina, 2006.

ISANTI

DAVID C. JOHNSON CIVIC ARENA

NOTES - This is a modern 1-rink facility built in 1997 for the Cambridge-Isanti Youth Hockey Association and High School, and North Branch Hockey Association.

David C. Johnson Civic Arena
600 1st Ave. N.
Isanti, MN 55040

763-444-6432

KASSON

DODGE COUNTY FOUR SEASONS ARENA

Dodge County Four Seasons Arena
100 11th St. N.E.
Kasson, MN 55944

507-634-2222

NOTES - The new rink built in 1996 is a contrast to the old building on the Dodge County Fairgrounds. This is the home ice for the Wildcats of Dodge County.

LA CRESCENT

La Crescent Community Arena
520 14th St. S.
La Crescent, MN 55947

507-895-4160

NOTES - This arena has the distinction of being located in the farthest southeast corner of the state. This arena was built in 1996 and has one rink.

This air hockey table, in the La Crescent Arena lobby, is a blast from the past. Though they can still be found today, they hit their peak of popularity back in the '70s.

84

A view from the bleachers in Rink 1.

A dad looks on during a practice in Ames Arena Rink 2.

Lakeville U14 A breaks out the puck in a game against Woodbury in Rink 1, February 2007.

Ames Arena
19900 Ipava Ave.
Lakeville, MN 55044

952-469-1248

NOTES - Built in 1994, this arena is located at the North High School and has two rinks. Rink 1 is Olympic size with Rink 2 measuring in at 190' X 85'.

The Pucks are chilled and ready to go.

Le Sueur Community Center
821 Ferry St. E.
Le Sueur, MN 56058

507-665-3325

NOTES - This is a 1-rink facility built in 1977 which services Le Sueur-Henderson-St. Peter High School Hockey.

Squirt players wait patiently to take a turn at a back-checking drill, March 2007.

Catching up with other hockey parents in the heated viewing area above the rink.

Chisago Lakes Arena
29400 Olinda Tr.
Lindstrom, MN 55045

651-257-8694

NOTES - Built in 1991 with one sheet, this arena provides ice for both Chisago Lakes and North Branch High Schools.

A view from the bleachers.

Litchfield Civic Arena
900 Gilman Ave. N.
Litchfield, MN 55355

320-693-2679

NOTES - This arena was constructed in 1973 by the town of Litchfield for the Litchfield-Dassel-Cokato High School and Youth Hockey Associations.

LITTLE FALLS

EXCHANGE ARENA

Younger siblings can usually find Sponge Bob or something good on the TV in the viewing area.

Exchange Arena
1001 5th Ave. S.E.
Little Falls, MN 56345

320-632-2032

NOTES - This 1-rink arena just southeast of Little Falls was constructed in 1988.

LONG PRAIRIE

TODD COUNTY EXPO ARENA

Todd County Expo Arena
2nd Ave. NE & 9th St. N.E.
Long Prairie, MN 56347

320-732-6015

A Mites practice, March 2007.

NOTES - The Todd County Expo Arena has one rink, was built in 1972 and is located at the Todd County Fairgrounds.

The sun sets on the arena in December, 2006.

Blue Mound Ice Arena
601 Hatting St. W.
Luverne, MN 56156

507-449-9138

NOTES - Luverne's Blue Mound Arena is unique geographically because it sits farthest southwest of all Minnesota arenas.

Quite the turnout in the stands for a District game.

Future stars look on. If you're not playing hockey in Luverne, you are probably watching it.

The silhoutte of a grain elevator behind the rink provides a peaceful rural setting.

A view into the office at the All Seasons Arena.

NOTES - All Seasons is the home of Mankato East and West High Schools and provides practice ice for Mankato State Womens and Mens Teams. The South Rink is standard size built in 1973 while the North Rink has larger 200' X 100' Olympic measurements and was finished in 1998. Notable players from this ice include Ryan Carter, Grant Stevenson and David Backes.

All Seasons Arena
1251 Monks Ave.
Mankato, MN 56003   507-387-6552

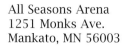

The South Rink during an Adult League game.

A post game handshake on the South Rink.

More old guys on the North Rink.

MANKATO

Brian Fowler

Mankato State takes on University of Minnesota.

Midwest Wireless Civic Center
One Civic Center Plaza
Mankato, MN 56001

507-389-3000

NOTES - Located in the heart of downtown Mankato, the Civic Center is the home ice for the Mens and Womens Mankato State Teams. The arena has seating capacty of 5000 and has an Olympic-size sheet.

93

MAPLE GROVE

Maple Grove Community Center
12951 Weaver Lake Rd.
Maple Grove, MN 55369

763-494-6465

MAPLE GROVE COMMUNITY CENTER

NOTES - This 1-rink facility was built in 1977 and seats 1100. It provides ice for Osseo-Maple Grove High School and Hockey Association. Maple Grove has plans to start building a second rink as this book comes out.

MARSHALL

LYON COUNTY ICE FACILITY

Lyon County Ice Facility
Hwy. 19 E. & Fairground Rd.
Marshall, MN 56258

507-537-6795

NOTES - Located at the fairgrounds, this is a single regulation rink facility built in 1995.

Figure skaters, January 2007.

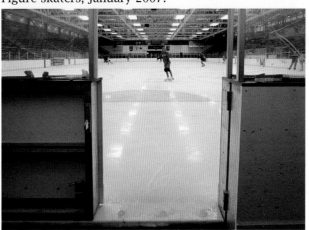

Aldrich Ice Arena
1850 White Bear Ave. N.
Maplewood, MN 55109

651-748-2510

NOTES - Aldrich Arena is a classic; built back in 1962, it seats a whopping 3400 spectators. It is the home ice for Hill-Murray High School.

NOTES - Saint Thomas Arena is the home of the St. Thomas Academy High School Cadets and the University of St. Thomas Tommies. It was opened in 2003 and seats 1400.

The University of St. Thomas Womens Team in action. Photo courtesy of the Saint Thomas Ice Arena website.

Saint Thomas Ice Arena
950 Mendota Heights Rd.
Mendota Heights, MN 55120

651-209-6020

This photo of the 2006 Class A State Championship Team is courtesy of the Saint Thomas Ice Arena website.

MINNEAPOLIS

AUGSBURG COLLEGE ICE ARENA

Augsburg Ice Arena
2323 Riverside Ave.
Minneapolis, MN 55454

612-330-1504

NOTES - This arena sits in urban Minneapolis on the Augsburg campus. It was built in 1972 and has two sheets of ice, the second rink with undersized measurments of 185' X 85'. The main rink plays host for Augsburg College and seats 600.

MINNEAPOLIS

THE DEPOT ICE RINK

The Depot
225 3rd Ave. S.
Minneapolis, MN 55401

612-339-2253

NOTES - This rink is attached to a Courtyard Residence Inn, and the whole group of buildings was once the old Milwaukee Railroad train depot. It is located in downtown Minneapolis and is a favorite rink for figure skating and open skating.

The picture above shows a crew removing the protective covering from the ice. The ice is not removed; it is covered for dry floor activities like conventions.

MINNEAPOLIS

Mariucci Arena
1901 4th St. S.E.
Minneapolis, MN 55455

612-625-5804

Mariucci sits on the University of Minnesota campus.

NOTES - Named after long-time former coach John Mariucci, this arena was completed in 1993, and the U of M Gophers moved from their old ice at Williams Arena, "the Barn", to this modern facility. It has Olympic-size ice and seats about 10,000. The championship banners hanging from the rafters show the success of this program. Local Association Teams like to rent practice ice here to get a chance to skate in the big house. Names of note would fill several pages so here is just a handful: Aaron, Paul and Neal Broten, Ken Yackel, Bill Baker, Brian Bonin, Scott Bjugstad, Chris McAlpine, Dave Snuggerude and legendary coach Herb Brooks.

MINNEHAHA ACADEMY ICE ARENA

Minnehaha Academy Ice Arena
4200 West River Pkwy.
Minneapolis, MN 55406

612-728-7788

NOTES - This arena is on the campus of
Minnehaha Acadamy private school which
overlooks the mighty Mississippi on West
River Road in Minneapolis. It is home for
both Boys and Girls High School Teams.

This is a cold rink with crowds usually first forming under the heaters.

A high school practice, February 2007.

In the locker room before a Squirt game.

Colorful people and colorful food can be found here.

Northeast Ice Arena
1306 Central Ave. N.E.
Minneapolis, MN 55418

612-782-2123

NOTES - Formerly Edison Ice Arena, this arena sits just north of downtown Minneapolis. It was built in 1997 and is home ice for Edison High School.

101

A Girls Section 6AA High School Playoff game, February 2007.

The Walker Sculpture Gardens.

NOTES - Parade has a nice view of the downtown Minneapolis skyline overlooking the Walker Sculpture Gardens. There are three sheets of ice here: two Olympic-size and a very small Studio Rink. The first, South Rink, was completed in 1973 and the North Rink, which seats 1200, added later. It is the home to the inner city High Schools, and the NHL Wild practice here.

Parade Ice Garden
600 Kenwood Pkwy.
Minneapolis, MN 55404

612-370-4846

Because the human eye filters it, the light in the South Rink appears to be white/normal, but there is actually quite a green cast which can be captured using photography.

The Women Gophers are perennial favorites.

The games are a favorite of youth girl players.

Just prior to the start of a Womens Gophers game in the rink's inaugural season of 2001.

Ridder Arena
1815 4th St. S.E.
Minneapolis, MN 55455

612-625-5804

NOTES - Sitting next to Mariucci on the U of M campus, this regulation-size arena was built in 2002 specifically as a home for the Women Gophers. Too numerous to mention all, some notable players include Natalie Darwitz, Krissy Wendell, Ronda Curtin and Winny Brodt.

MINNEAPOLIS

VICTORY MEMORIAL ICE ARENA

Victory Memorial Ice Arena
1900 42nd Ave. N.
Minneapolis, MN 55412

612-668-2230

NOTES - This arena was built
in 1974 with a standard size
sheet for the North
Minneapolis High School and
Association Hockey.

Rink A during a Minnetonka and Edina Junior Gold game, 2007.

Rink B just underwent a facelift, and is now a sporty red, white and blue.

Minnetonka Ice Arena
3401 Williston Rd.
Minnetonka, MN 55345

952-939-8310

NOTES - Rink A was built in 1968 and B added later. They provided all the ice for the Minnetonka High School Team until the Pagel Arena was built. Hopkins High School also skates here.

105

MINNETONKA

The ice rink is part of a larger athletic facility and there is running track that goes around the rink which provides viewing options for spectators.

Pagel Activity Center
18313 Hwy. 7
Minnetonka, MN 55345

952-470-4099

NOTES - The Pagel sits right behind Minnetonka High School and is a 1-sheet facility recently completed in about 2001.

A view from the running track above the player boxes at the conclusion of a Girls High School game in 2007.

107

Moose Sherritt Ice Arena
800 Broadway E.
Monticello, MN 58362

763-271-0885

NOTES - This arena, which was completed in 2006, provides ice for the Monticello, Annandale and Maple Lake High School Teams and Youth Associations. The rink is known as "The Moose".

Power plant steam makes locating Monticello easy.

Moose Sherritt memorabilia fills a display case.

The North Rink during a Peewee game.

South Rink during open skating, February 2007.

Moorhead Sports Center
324 24th St. S.
Moorhead, MN 56560

218-299-5354

NOTES - Moorhead Sports Center has two sheets, both regulation size. The South Rink was completed in 1974, seats 3000, and acts as the home for Moorhead High School as well as Concordia College.

109

MOORHEAD   MOORHEAD YOUTH HOCKEY ARENA

The North Rink during a tournament game.

The lobby is hopping with hockey commerce.

The South Rink has bleachers but also great viewing from above.

Moorhead Youth Hockey Arena
707 Main Ave. S.E.
Moorhead, MN 56560

218-233-5021

NOTES - The MHYH Arena is a 2-sheet venue completed in 1998. The larger North Rink seats 1000.

A little guy cheers on his brother during some street hockey in the hallways.

In March of 2007, with the High School and Association Hockey seasons completed, there is extra ice for those who want to start working on next year.

Riverside Arena
Hwy. 27 & Arrowhead Ln.
Moose Lake, MN 55767

218-485-4280

NOTES - Riverside Arena is a single-sheet arena built in 1986 for the High School and Association Hockey.

111

The arena is easy to find; simply make your way to the big horse, then turn into the fairgrounds.

District playoff time means large crowds.

Mora Civic Center
701 Union St. S.
Kanabec County Fairgrounds
Mora, MN 55051

320-679-2443

NOTES - This rink is a single-sheet arena built in 1988 and provides ice for Mora/Hinckley High School and Association Hockey.

Like most rinks, heat is provided only where needed.

Lee Community Center
County Rd. 22
Morris, MN 56267

320-589-4585

NOTES - This is a nice new arena which opened in 1994, and serves as ice for the Morris-Benson Storm High School and Association Hockey.

113

MOUND

DAVID M. THALER SPORTS CENTER

David M. Thaler Sports Center
5909 Sunnyfield Rd. E.
Mound, MN 55364

952-491-8277

The Boys HS Team gears up for playoffs, Feb. 2007.

NOTES - This arena was just completed and sits next to the Mound West Tonka High School.

MOUND

HAROLD J. POND SPORTS CENTER

Harold J. Pond Sports Center
2121 Commerce Blvd.
Mound, MN 55364

952-472-6565

NOTES - This 1-sheet arena sits in downtown Mound and was built in 1981 for Mound and Orono High School and Associations.

NASHWAUK

NASHWAUK RECREATION COMPLEX

NOTES - This Iron Range rink was built in 1980 and serves Nashwauk and Chisholm.

The rink is just down the hill from the water tower.

Nashwauk Recreation Complex
301 Central Ave.
Nashwauk, MN 55769

218-885-1210

NEW HOPE

NEW HOPE ICE ARENA

NOTES - This is a 2-sheet arena, with the North Rink completed in 1975 and South Rink added later. It is home ice for Cooper, Armstrong and Robbinsdale High Schools.

The concession area overlooks the South Rink.

New Hope Ice Arena
4949 Louisiana Ave. N.
New Hope, MN 55428

763-531-5181

Viewing the North Rink which seats 2200.

115

New Prague Area Comm. Center
100 12th St. N.W.
New Prague, MN 56071

952-758-7825

NOTES - This is a newer arena built in 1996 for New Prague High School and Association as well as Montgomery Hockey Association.

The North Arena is regulation size.

The commons area between the two rinks.

Mite Hockey on the South Arena which is Olympic size and seats 1000.

New Ulm Civic Center
1212 Franklin St. N
New Ulm, MN 56073

507-233-8400

NOTES - New Ulm Civic Center is an impressive new complex just completed in 2003 with two rinks–one NHL regulation-size and an Olympic sheet. The rink replaces the old Vogle Arena which opened in 1981 and was built with proceeds from a 1/2 cent sales tax referendum. It is home ice for the New Ulm Eagles.

OK, so this isn't next to the rink, but the North St. Paul Snowman needed to make an appearance.

The original 1960's ticket window.

The ice waits for the Varsity game on next.

Polar Arena
2520 11th Ave. E.
North St. Paul, MN 55109

651-748-6292

NOTES - This rink was built back in 1969 and sits next to North High School. When the Polars play and fill this arena to its 1200 person capacity, it gets intense.

NORTHFIELD

CITY OF NORTHFIELD ARENA

Where the magic happens–the skate sharpening that is.

City of Northfield Arena
1280 Bollenbacher Dr.
Northfield, MN 55057

507-645-3017

NOTES - This 1-sheet arena was completed in 1972 and seats 741. Carleton College, St. Olaf College and Northfield High School all skate here.

OAKDALE

TARTAN ARENA

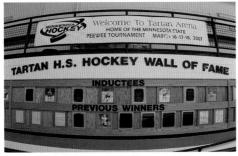

Like many arenas, there is a Wall of Fame.

Tartan Arena
740 Greenway Ave. N.
Oakdale, MN 55128

651-714-9251

NOTES - Tartan Arena is located at the High School and serves as ice for both the Girls and Boys Teams.

ORONO

NOTES - Sitting next to the High School, this one Olympic-size rink was built in 1997 and seats 1200.

ORONO ICE ARENA

Orono Ice Arena
1025 Old Crystal Bay Rd.
Orono, MN 55356

952-449-6090

A view from the clock box.

OSSEO

Osseo-Park Ice Arena
10390 County Rd. 81
Osseo, MN 55369

763-425-7306

OSSEO-PARK ICE ARENA

NOTES - You can't miss this rink, just hop on 81 in Osseo and you will see it. It was built in 1995 with two regulation-size rinks to service Osseo and Brooklyn Center.

OWATONNA

FOUR SEASONS CENTER

Better rinks through advertising revenue.

The locker room just before a U10 game.

A dad shows some team spirit at a Peewee Tournament game in Rink 1.

The rink sits southeast of
downtown, on the fairgrounds.

Four Seasons Center
1525 Elm Ave. S.
Owatonna, MN 55060

507-451-1093

NOTES - This is a 2- sheet arena with Rink 1
being built in 1973 and having non-regulation measurements of 190' X 85'. It seats a
sizable crowd of 1400.

121

After the High School and Association seasons conclude, there is plenty of ice for open skating until the rink shuts down in March.

Ted O. Johnson Ice Arena
211 Huntsinger Ave.
Park Rapids, MN 56470

218-732-9179

NOTES - Built in the '80s, this is a 1-regulation rink arena, seating 700, and is home to the Park Rapids Panthers.

The bleachers are Park Rapids orange and black.

Mites provide entertainment on a Saturday morning in February 2007.

NOTES - The Koronis Arena has one sheet, was built in 1992 for Paynesville-New London-Spicer Hockey Association, and is home ice for River Lakes High School Hockey.

Koronis Civic Arena
28780 Koronis Dr.
Paynesville, MN 56362

320-243-3710

PINE CITY

Korbel Arena
1225 Main St. S.
Pine City, MN 55063

320-629-7512

KORBEL ARENA

NOTES - Korbel is a 1-sheet facility completed in 1999. The photo above was taken in March at the conclusion of the season, and shows the early stages of "taking out the ice". There is a system: first the lines need to be edged out, then the remaining ice down to the concrete needs to be scraped up and physically removed.

PLYMOUTH

NOTES - This is a 3-sheet complex, with Rink A (Olympic-size seating 1000) and Rink B (regulation-size seating 200) both being built in 1997. Rink C is regulation-size seating 500 and was completed in 2004. Notable players include Jordan Leopold and Matt Hussey.

PLYMOUTH ICE CENTER

Plymouth Ice Center
3650 Plymouth Blvd.
Plymouth, MN 55446

762-509-5250

The locker rooms for the Olympic rink have a unique triangular shape which makes for close quarters.

PLYMOUTH

Wayzata Ice Arena
305 Vicksburg Ln.
Plymouth, MN 55447

763-745-6018

NOTES - The Wayzata Ice Arena was built back in 1972, has a single sheet and sits behind the High School.

Wayzata youth hockey uses this ice extensively.

WAYZATA ICE ARENA

Varsity players cheer as Edina Girls JV scores in an end-of-season Tournament game against Benilde, February 2007.

PRINCETON

NOTES - This 1-rink arena was completed in 1981 as the home for Princeton High School and Youth Hockey.

Concessions and ice are prepared for a Princeton Boys High School game in February 2007.

PRINCETON ARENA

Princeton Ice Arena
511 Ice Arena Dr.
Princeton, MN 55271

320-389-5142

125

The championship medal ceremony at a U10 Hockey Tournament in 2002.

Dakotah Sports & Fitness
2100 Trail of Dreams
Prior Lake, MN 55372

952-496-6864

NOTES - This rink, in the multi-sport center at Mystic Lake, was built in 1994 and seats 900. Locating it is easy on a dark winter night; just go to the lasers which shine up into the sky from Mystic Lake Casino in the form of a giant Teepee. Dakotah is owned and operated by the Mdewakanton Sioux Community.

The lobby opens to the sports center.

The 92Xtreme AAA Girls Hockey Team runs through some system drills during a practice in July 2007.

Rails support is everywhere.

The Proctor Girls High School Team practices in January 2007.

Proctor Arena
800 Boundary Ave. N.
Proctor, MN 55810

218-624-7988

NOTES - This rink was built in 1975 and has one sheet of ice measuring in slightly short at 191' X 85'. The locals are proud of their Rails.

It's a little quiet on a March night in 2007 after the conclusion of hockey season.

Cardin-Hunt Arena
Bridge Street NW
Red Lake Falls, MN 56750

218-253-2034

NOTES - This arena is a classic and was built back in 1965 with ice dimensions of 193' X 85'.

This tightly packed arena, with seats built right into the walls, has a surprisingly large seating capacity of 800.

A Peewee district game in February 2007.

Bergwall Arena
306 Pioneer Rd.
Red Wing, MN 56368

320-597-7522

NOTES - This is a 1-sheet facility built in
1999 for the Red Wing High School Teams
and Association.

129

Boys High School Sections draws a large crowd in February 2007.

Prairie Island Arena
370 Guernsey Ln.
Red Wing, MN 55066

651-380-9663

NOTES - Prairie Island Arena is located at
the High School and was built in 1999
specifically for the High School Teams.

The Zamboni drains between resurfacing.

Redwood Area Civic Arena
901 Cook St.
Redwood Falls, MN 56283

507-644-2333

NOTES - Recently built in 2000, this is a
single-regulation rink seating 500.

RICHFIELD

Hat Trick Hockey Store is located in the arena.

Richfield Rink 2.

Richfield Ice Arena
636 66th St. E.
Richfield, MN 55423

612-861-9351

NOTES - Richfield Ice Arena has two sheets. The first was built in 1971 seats 1800; and the second was built in 1999 and seats 200. This is the home ice for Richfield and Holy Angels High School Hockey. NHL players from this arena include Steve Christoff, Darby Hendrickson, Al Ness, Damian Rhodes, Brett Hauer and Jim Branch.

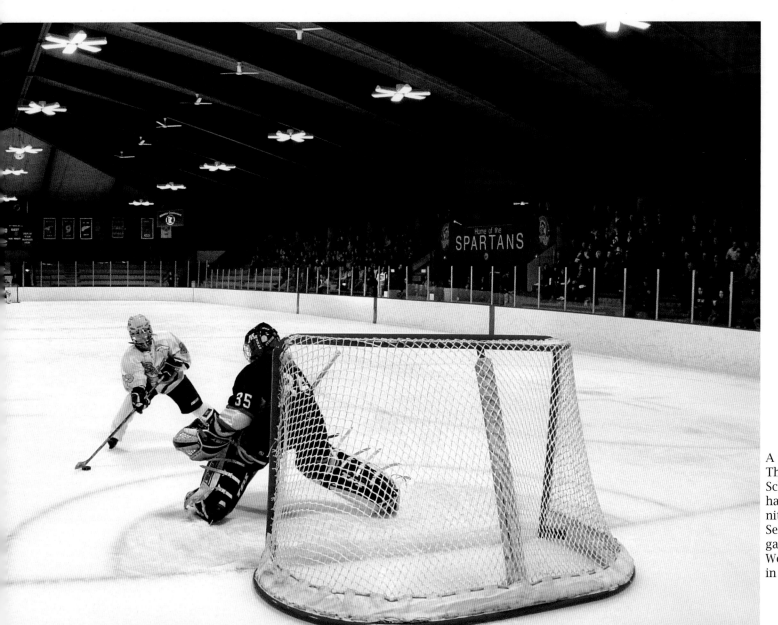

A penalty shot. The Breck High School Girls Team has a rare opportunity during a Section Playoff game with Mound-Westonka in Rink 1 in 2007.

133

The ice is made ready for the next batch getting dropped off.

River Lakes Civic Arena
319 Central Ave. S.
Richmond, MN 56368

320-597-7522

NOTES - This arena has one regulation-size rink and was built in 1996. It provides ice for the River Lake High School Stars, St. John's University, College of St. Benedict and Cold Springs Hockey Association.

A face-off in Graham 2.

Graham 1 during a Bantam Tournament in 2006. It seats 1900.

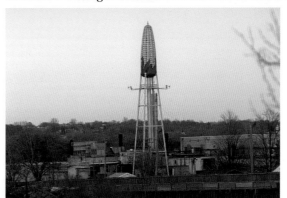

Directions: Find the corn on the cob fairgrounds water tower, then head towards the swine barn.

NOTES - The first rink here was built in 1969; Graham 2 was added in 1984; Graham 3 in 1989; and Graham 4 was just completed in 2007. This facility provides ice for Rochester Lourdes and Mayo High Schools as well as the local Association. Local players of note include Doug Zmolek, Sjhon Podein and Mark Stewart. In Minnesota, only the Blaine Super Rink has more sheets of ice than Graham.

Graham Arena
200 Arena Dr.
Rochester, MN 55904

507-281-6189

The Rochester Figure Skating Club is a heavy user of Olmsted North Rink.

Olmsted Recreation Center
21 Elton Hills Dr. N.W.
Rochester, MN 55901

507-281-6168

NOTES - This arena was built in 1975 with two regulation rinks. The larger Hoffman Rink seats over 2500 and provides ice for Rochester John Marshall and Century High Schools.

The growing youth population in the area keeps the rink busy.

Rogers Activity Center
21080 141st. Ave. N.
Rogers, MN 55374

763-428-1033

NOTES - The RAC is a new 1-regulation-size rink, seating 500 in a comfortable modern building.

The Memorial Arena during a District Peewee game.

In Roseau, the arena is the place to be.

The North Rink has reduced dimensions of 180' X 60' and standing viewing only.

Roseau Memorial Arena
315 3rd Ave. N.E.
Roseau, MN 56751

218-463-1538

NOTES - The Memorial Arena is a great classic hockey venue built back in 1949. It can accommodate 2500 fans for those big Roseau High School Hockey games. The small town of Roseau is second only to Edina in collecting Boys State High School Championships.

ROSEMOUNT COMMUNITY CENTER

The Rosemount Girls High School Hockey Team observes the national anthem just prior to a game in 2006.

They are proud of their Irish High School Hockey here.

Rosemount Community Center
13885 Robert Trail S.
Rosemount, MN 55068

651-322-6006

NOTES - This arena was completed in 1993 as a home for the Rosemount High School and Association Teams. It has one regulation rink that seats 1200. The USA Broomball National Championships have been held on this ice. Local players of note include Tom Preising (LA Kings, San Jose Sharks, Ottowa Senators) and Tim Conboy (San Jose Sharks, Carolina Hurricanes).

Roseville Skating Center
2661 Civic Center Dr.
Roseville, MN 55113

651-729-7007

The Roseville Figure Skating Club uses the indoor rink on a cold January evening in 2007.

NOTES - Roseville Skating Center is also the home of the John Rose Minnesota Oval which is an outdoor refrigerated Olympic-size speed skating track. Olympic Tryouts have been held at this venue. The Skating Center has one indoor rink which was built back in 1969 for Roseville High School and seats 2000. Skaters of note from this rink include: Marty Sertich (MN Mr. Hockey and Hobey Baker Winner 2005), Chris McAlpine & Steve Griffith (1984 US Olympians), Winny Brodt (MN Ms. Hockey & US Team), Chelsea Brodt (MN Ms. Hockey), Renee Curtin (MN Ms. Hockey), and Rhonda Curtin (MN Ms. Hockey). The Oval boasts 110,000 square feet of refrigerated ice -THAT'S HUGE!

The John Rose Oval.

SARTELL

BERNICK'S PEPSI ARENA

Bernick's Pepsi Arena
1109 1st St. S.
Sartell, MN 56377

320-240-9233

NOTES - Bernick's Pepsi Arena is a newly completed regulation-size rink seating 300.

SAUK CENTRE

SAUK CENTRE CIVIC ARENA

NOTES - This single-regulation-sheet arena was built in 1994 for the High School team and seats 1200. It's located in town atop the hill by the water tower.

Sauk Centre Civic Arena
818 Centre St.
Sauk Centre, MN 56378

320-352-1271

A tournament is running late as these Peewee players watch and wait for the game before theirs to end.

Sports Arena East
1410 3rd Ave. S.
Sauk Rapids, MN 56379

320-252-0508

NOTES - This is a 1-sheet arena built in 1986 and seats 750. It provides ice for many teams including Sauk Rapids and Sartell High Schools as well as Sartell, Sauk Rapids and St. Cloud Youth Hockey.

SHAKOPEE COMMUNITY CENTER

Shakopee Community Center Ice Arena during a Girls High School Varsity game in 2006.

Shakopee Community Center Ice Arena
1255 Fuller St.
Shakopee, MN 55379

952-233-9522

NOTES - The Shakopee Arena was built in 1995, has a regulation sheet, is open year 'round and seats 1000.

Shoreview Arena
877 West Hwy. 96
Shoreview, MN 55126

651-766-4000

NOTES - Shoreview Arena is one of the
many Ramsey County arenas built in the
'70s. This one was completed in 1974, has
a single regulation-size rink, seats 200, and
provides ice for Moundsview and Irondale.

The red accent is used in most of the
Ramsey County arenas.

NOTES - Rukavina Arena was one of two built back in 1966 from the same drawings, the other being down the road in Two Harbors. They share the same shape but each arena definitely takes care of its own decorating.

I can't quite make out what that green one on the top shelf reads.

This is home ice for the Silver Bay High School Mariners.

Rukavina Arena
129 Outer Dr.
Silver Bay, MN 55614

218-226-4214

145

Rukavina Arena in Silver Bay
from the lobby/viewing room.

SLEEPY EYE

Scenes from the arena during a Peewee game in February 2007.

Sleepy Eye Arena
620 Southdale St. S.W.
Sleepy Eye, MN 56085

507-794-5406

NOTES - Sleepy Eye Arena was built in 1994 with one regulation sheet, and seats 650 in some very colorful chairs.

Rink 2.

South St. Paul Boys High School Team practices on Rink 1.

Wakota Civic Arena
141 6th St. S.
South St. Paul, MN 55075

651-554-3330

NOTES - Wakota's Rink 1 was completed in 1962 and can seat up to 3400. This 2-sheet facility is the home for the always strong South St. Paul High School and Association Teams.

149

St. Cloud Cathedral High School Boys Team practices on the Dave Torrey Arena.

Ritsche Arena was added in 1997.

Municipal Athletic Complex
5001 8th St. N.
St. Cloud, MN 56303

320-255-7223

NOTES - The MAC is a multi-sport complex with two regulation sheets. The first Dave Torrey Arena, was constructed in 1972 and seats 1800. It is home to St. Cloud Tech, and Apollo, and Cathedral High School Hockey Teams. The St. Cloud High School Girls Ice Breakers and St. Ben's College Womens as well as the Granite City Lumberjack AAA Teams also use the ice here.

Starting line-up, April 2003.

Rink 1 seats 5600.

National Hockey Center
1204 4th Ave. S.
St. Cloud, MN 56301

320-255-3327

NOTES - The National Hockey Center has two Olympic-size rinks and was built in 1989. It is home to St. Johns University, the D1 St. Cloud State Huskies and St. Cloud Tech High School. NHL Players from this arena include: Mark Parish, Brett Hedican, Matt Cullen, Joe Motsko, Lenny Esau, Mark Hardigan, Tyler Arneson, Ryan Malone, Duvey Wescott, Jeff Meyer and Jeff Finger. This arena may look familiar because it was a backdrop for the movie *The Mighty Ducks*.

The South U10 Team fires up prior to competing in the Minnesota Selects AAA Tournament, held here each April.

151

The West Arena during a U14 A District Playoff game between Minnetonka and Edina.

The West Arena from the bleachers.

The East Arena between periods.

St. Louis Park Rec. Center
3700 Monterey Dr.
St. Louis Park, MN 55416

952-924-2540

NOTES - The Rec. Center was built back in 1970 and has two regulation sheets. The West Arena seats 2000 and is the home ice for St. Louis Park and Benilde High Schools.

ST. MARY'S POINT

ST. MARY'S POINT ICE ARENA

A St. Mary's Point Youth Hockey Association practice in February of 2007.

St. Mary's Point Ice Arena
2489 Itasca Ave. S.
St. Mary's Point, MN 55043

NOTES - This rink was built in 1968 with a non-regulation sheet measuring 185' X 85'. The seating here maxes out at 100.

The bleachers here get you very close to the action.

These guys take a break from their Showcase Hockey practice to pose for the camera.

Biff Adams Arena
743 Western Ave. N.
St. Paul, MN 55103

651-558-2200

NOTES - Located near downtown St. Paul, this arena was one of the many Ramsey County arenas built in the '70s. This one was finished in 1974 with one regulation sheet and provides ice for Como High School.

Like many of the Ramsey County rinks, it's a modest arena.

CHARLES M. SCHULTZ HIGHLAND ARENA

Skating lessons here are very popular.

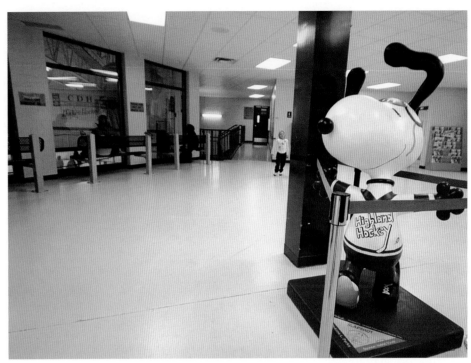

The Schultz Highland Arena wouldn't be complete without a *Peanuts* character.

Charles Schultz Highland Arena
800 Snelling Ave. S.
St. Paul, MN 55116

651-695-3766

NOTES - Just go to the top of the hill by the tower to find this rink. It has two sheets, was built in 1978 and is home ice for Cretin-Durham Hall High School Hockey.

155

A Youth Association game in January 2007.

Drake Arena
1712 Randolph Ave.
St. Paul, MN 55105

651-696-1346

NOTES - Drake Arena is located at St. Paul Academy and is a 1-regulation-sheet facility. It is home ice for SPA and also Hamline University.

The extra locker rooms are "no frills".

Similar to many Ramsey County arenas, this one shares the red and white color scheme.

Gustafson/Phalen Arena
1320 Walsh St.
St. Paul, MN 55106

651-772-6161

NOTES - This 1-regulation-sheet arena was built back in 1973 and sits right behind Johnson High School.

There are three items you can always find for sale at an ice rink: tape, laces and mouthguards.

Harding Arena
1496 6th St. E.
St. Paul, MN 55106

651-772-6190

NOTES - Harding Arena is home ice for Harding High School Hockey and Youth Hockey Association. It is a 1-regulation-size rink seating 300 and was built by Ramsey County in 1973.

The arena was dedicated to local boy Ken Yackel who went on to achieve many great things, and give back so much to the hockey world.

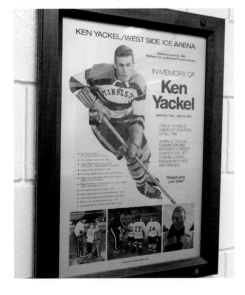

Ken Yackel West Side Arena
44 Isabel St. E.
St. Paul, MN 55107

651-215-0000

NOTES - This is another single-sheet Ramsey County rink complete with the original 1973 boards. It is located just minutes southeast of downtown St. Paul.

159

State Fair Coliseum
1784 Judson Ave.
St. Paul, MN 55108

651-642-2204

Just a portion of the floor area is filled by the rink, as the Coliseum is used for many dry floor events including livestock shows during the Minnesota State Fair, held every summer.

NOTES - In Minnesota, if you have a large summertime-use building with seating, it's only logical that it should be used as an ice rink in the winter. There is one regulation-size rink here, which was completed in 1973 and has seating capacity of 5250.

Oscar Johnson Arena
1039 Decourcy Cir.
St. Paul, MN 55105

651-643-3000

NOTES - Located in Energy Park, this is a 1-regula-
tion-size rink completed in 1971 and is another
Ramsey County arena.

Bring something warm, it's
always chilly in Oscar Johnson.

Skating lessons are well attended at Pleasant Arena as indicated by this crowd on a Saturday morning in January 2007.

Pleasant Arena
848 Pleasant Ave.
St. Paul, MN 55102

651-215-9030

NOTES - This arena was built in 1973 by Ramsey County with one regulation sheet. It seats 300.

ST. PAUL

XCEL ENERGY CENTER

Every seat at the Xcel is a good one.

Xcel Energy Center
199 Kellogg Blvd. W.
St. Paul, MN 55102

651-726-8160

NOTES - This is the home of the NHL Minnesota Wild. This facility was finished in 2000 and has sold out its 18,600 seats for every home game since that time. It also plays host to the Minnesota State High School Hockey Tournament and sells out for those games, as well.

This is the location of the former Civic Center.

The national anthem plays during a home game in the inaugural season, 2000.

The "Puck Wall" display in the lobby allows anyone to be a part of this rink's history, for a small fee.

North Dakota fans cheer during the "Frozen Five" at the Xcel Center. In this photo the Fighting Sioux take a one-goal lead over the St. Cloud State Huskies on March 16, 2007.

ST. PETER

LUND ICE ARENA

Open skating is a warm alternative to outdoor exercise for students on this cold February morning.

Gustavus sits atop the hill in St. Peter.

Lund Ice Arena
800 College Ave. W.
St. Peter, MN 56082

507-933-7615

NOTES - Located on campus, this rink was built in 1974 as home ice for Gustavus Adolphus College, and seats 1200. St. Peter-Le Sueur Youth Hockey also uses the ice.

The arena is connected to other campus buildings.

That's no special effect; the glass behind the goals shows some serious mileage.

NOTES - Lily Lake has served the Stillwater area since 1971. The ice is slightly under regulation at 196' X 85' and seating capacity is 700. Stillwater and Mahtomedi High Schools use the ice here.

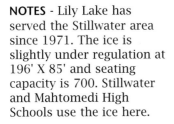

Lily Lake Arena
1208 Greeley St. S.
Stillwater, MN 55082

651-439-1248

St. Croix Rec. Center
1675 Market Dr.
Stillwater, MN 55082

651-430-2601

NOTES - The South Rink was built in 1998 with seating for 1300, and the North was built in 2000 with seating for 300. Stillwater and Mahtomedi High School Teams use this ice. Former NCAA MVP and current Detroit Red Wing Adam Berkhoel is from here.

168

The South Rink seats 3000.

Viewing in the North Rink is from above.

THIEF RIVER FALLS

HUCK OLSON MEMORIAL CIVIC CENTER

Huck Olson Memorial Civic Center
501 Brooks Ave.
Thief River Falls, MN 56701

218-683-7243

NOTES - This 3450-seat, single-sheet arena opened in 1969, and served as the main hockey venue in this area until the new Ralph Engelstad Arena opened next door.

169

THIEF RIVER FALLS

RALPH ENGELSTAD ARENA

The lobby has the "Vegas" feel.

Ralph Engelstad Arena
525 Brooks Ave. N.
Thief River Falls, MN 56701

218-681-2183

NOTES - This impressive 13 million dollar arena was built in 2002 by the multi-millionaire Las Vegas hotel businessman and local, Ralph Engelstad. Ralph is known for donating to the Ralph Engelstad Arena at the University of North Dakota. There was controversy because he didn't like the idea of the University changing the Fighting Sioux name, so he had the name and logo put everywhere in the arena during construction, and threatened to discontinue financial backing if they ever changed the name or logo.

This "Ralph" has, in addition to a great hockey rink, a training center and a 5000-square-foot community room. The impression when entering this arena is that you are walking into some NHL franchise home rink.

The concessions and concourse add to the experience.

This arena is known as the "Mini Ralph", only because its namesake built an even grander arena at his alma mater University of North Dakota. It holds 3530, however that includes the over 280 bar stools on the concourse level. In this picture the place looks empty even though this game, in February of 2007, has drawn more than 100 spectators.

TWO HARBORS

LAKE COUNTY ARENA

Lake County Arena
301 8th. Ave.
Two Harbors, MN 55616

218-834-8339

NOTES - Built in 1966, this is a 1-sheet arena, and if you look back to the Silver Bay Arena, you can see the similar building layout, but a different color scheme, as these buildings are from the same drawing.

VICTORIA

VICTORIA FIELD HOUSE

Victoria Field House
8475 Kochia Ln.
Victoria, MN 55386

952-443-3140

NOTES - This is a new 1-sheet arena which opened several years ago. The Field House is a combined hockey arena and health club, and an indoor running track circles the ice rink.

VIRGINIA

MINERS MEMORIAL BUILDING

Miners Memorial Building
9th Ave. S.
Virginia, MN 55792

218-741-3583

NOTES - Virginia is located just north of Eveleth, home of the Hockey Hall of Fame, and is in the heart of the Iron Range. This is a classic arena built in 1959, with seating for 2500, and a second rink in the back.

WADENA

WADENA COMMUNITY CENTER

NOTES - There is one regulation sheet of ice at this arena, and it is home for the Wadena Wolverine High School Hockey Team as well as the local Youth Hockey Association.

Wadena Community Center
700 Community Center Dr.
Wadena, MN 56482

218-631-3031

The Gardens is an impressive arena, one you would expect to find in "Hockey Town" USA.

The Gardens
707 Elk St. N.W.
Warroad, MN 56763

218-386-3862

NOTES - This is a privately owned arena built in 1993 for the always strong Warroad High School Team.

The lobby is a busy place.

The Olympic Arena pictured above is the orignal rink at this facility. It sits to the right of the Gardens, but inconsistent with the name, the ice measurements are smaller than regulation at 190' X 85'.

The stands are packed for this Squirt game in January 2007.

Waseca Community Arena
1501 2nd St. N.W.
Waseca, MN 56093

507-835-3251

NOTES - This is a single regulation rink built in 1994 for the High School and local Association and seats 500 people.

175

Even practice is good entertainment when viewing from the warm lobby.

It's not an Olympic-size rink. These Mites are so small, they make the ice look very large.

West St. Paul Arena
60 West Emerson
West St. Paul, MN 55118

651-552-4155

NOTES - The West St. Paul Arena has one regulation rink that was built in 1971 and seats 500.

Look closely at the "open on top" locker rooms tucked to the right side of the arena.

White Bear Arena
2160 Orchard Ln.
White Bear Lake, MN 55110

651-748-2515

NOTES - This is another red and white Ramsey County Arena. It is a single regulation, bare bones rink built in 1973.

WHITE BEAR LAKE

WHITE BEAR HIPPODROME

White Bear Hippodrome
4855 Bloom Ave.
White Bear Lake, MN 55110

651-407-7508

NOTES - The Hippodrome is one of the oldest remaining arenas built back in 1924. It has seating for just 50 and measures in at a very small 180' X 66'. It was natural ice until 1991 when its first refrigeration system was installed. The movie *Ice Castles* was filmed in this rink.

It feels a little like the Twilight Zone when you enter this arena.

WHITE BEAR LAKE

WHITE BEAR LAKE SPORTS CENTER

A WBL Girls JV game at the Sports Center, January 2007.

The Sports Center is complete with weight room and skating treadmill.

NOTES - This arena was converted from a tennis center to a 1-regulation-sheet rink seating 300 in 1989. It is home to WBL Youth Hockey and the WBL Girls High School Team. Notable players skating here and at the Hippodrome include: NHL Hall of Famers Doc Romnes and Moose Goheen, Hobey Baker Award-winner Ryan Carter who is a member of the 2007 Stanley Cup Champion Mighty Ducks, Brian Bonin of the Wild and Bill Butters who played for both the MN Fighting Saints and MN North Stars.

White Bear Lake Sports Center
1328 Hwy. 96
White Bear Lake, MN 55110

651-429-8571

Watching dad play from the heated lobby.

Some serious action in an adult league.

Williams Ice Arena
525 Pine St.
Williams, MN 56686

218-783-3271

NOTES - Williams Ice Arena is a
1-regulation-sheet facility built in
1993 for the Baudette Youth
Hockey Association.

Skating lessons are in full swing on this Saturday morning in January 2007.

Willmar Civic Center
2707 Civic Center Dr.
Willmar, MN 56201

320-235-1454

NOTES - Built in 1979 by the City of Willmar, this 1-sheet arena seats 1500 and is home to Willmar High School Hockey.

WINDOM

WINDOM CITY ARENA

Rodeo fences and barrels sit in the back behind the rinks, awaiting next summer.

Windom City Arena
1480 8th Ave.
Windom, MN 56101

507-831-6122

Taking the ice at a Windom Bantam District game in January 2007.

An extremely narrow but long practice sheet is tucked in behind the main rink.

NOTES - The City Arena was built in 1979, seats 2500 and is located right on the Cottonwood County Fairgrounds. In the summer, the arena building holds horse shows, tractor pulls and other activities. There are two sheets of ice here, one regulation and another smaller practice rink.

These campers stretch before the morning session at Peak Performance Hockey Camp in June 2004.

Bud King Ice Arena
604 Front St.
Winona, MN 55987

507-454-7775

NOTES - Completed in 1987, this arena is home to Winona High School Hockey. It runs year 'round with most of the summer ice being used by Peak Performance Hockey Camp. Campers will get to know this rink well, as they will be on this ice three or four times a day for six days in a row.

183

WINONA

ST. MARY'S UNIVERSITY ARENA

St. Mary's University Arena
700 Terrace Heights
Winona, MN 55987

507-454-1412

NOTES - SMU Arena is tucked up against the bluffs at the back of campus. It is a 1-sheet facility completed in the '80s for DIII St. Mary's Cardinals.

WOODBURY

BIELENBERG SPORTS CENTER

Bielenberg Sports Center
4125 Radio Drive
Woodbury, MN 55125

651-714-3740

NOTES - Bielenberg has two regulation rinks; the West was built in 1995 seating 1100, and the East in 1998 seating 300. This arena is part of a larger athletic facility with attached covered field house dome.

A Bantam District 6 Playoff game gets started on the West Rink in February 2006.

This view looks west from the front of the rink on a peaceful January evening in 2007.

Anyone for some broom ball?

Worthington Ice Arena
1600 Stower Dr.
Worthington, MN 56187

507-376-2202

NOTES - This arena is located in the far south-west corner of Minnesota. It was built in 1980, has a single regulation sheet which seats 500, and is home of the Worthington Trojans.

185

PARTING SHOT - Chaska Rink A is ready and waiting.

GREATER MINNESOTA ARENA LOCATIONS AND CONCENTRATION

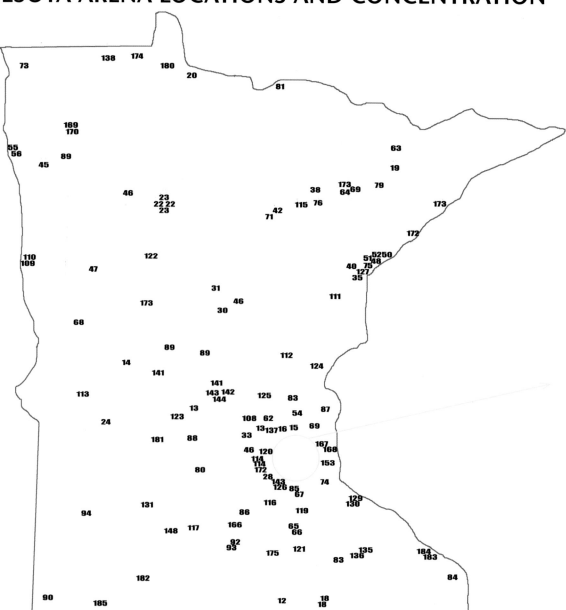

The number on the map is the page number for each arena in this book.

Note the concentrations up by the Canadian border, the Iron Range and, of course, the Metro Area with the large population base.

METRO AREA ARENA LOCATIONS AND CONCENTRATION

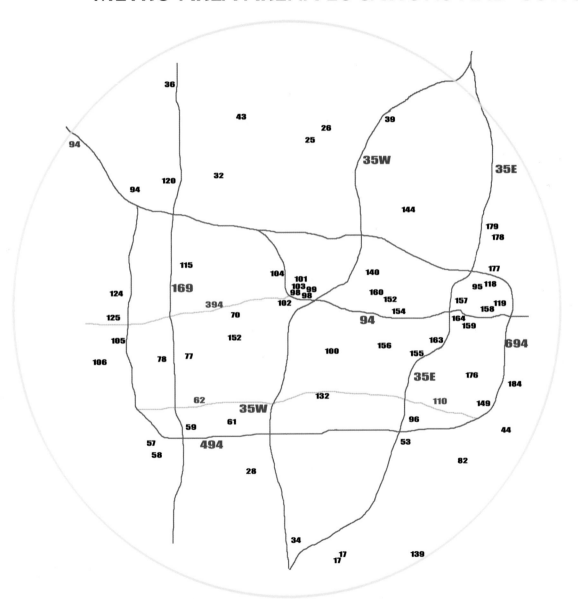

Depending on how it's defined, the Metro Area contains about 100 of the 173 indoor ice arenas in the state of Minnesota.

ABOUT THE PHOTOGRAPHER/AUTHOR

Photographer, hockey dad and coach Mike Krieter lives in Edina with his wife and three children. He has a strong hockey tradition which started with playing youth hockey himself in Edina, and eventually coaching all three of his children for a number of years.

Mike has been shooting commercial photos since 1990, specializing in people and action. His photography has captured numerous industry awards including: Communication Arts Photo Annual, Graphis, The One Show, Photo District News and Photographers Forum Magazine. Fine art competition awards include the People's Choice Awards at the Lyn/Lake Art Festival and second place at the Minnesota State Fair Fine Arts Competition. His photos have been seen in the following magazines: Outside, Woman's Health and Fitness, Minnesota Monthly, Mpls/St.Paul, Swing, Guideposts, Shareholder Value, Presentations, and Silent Sports. Clients include: McDonalds, Northwest Airlines, General Mills, Wells Fargo, Salomon, Caterpillar, TREX Decking and Blue Cross/Blue Shield.